HISTORY·IN·STONE

ANCIENT ROME

PHILIP STEELE

SilverDolphin

San Diego, California

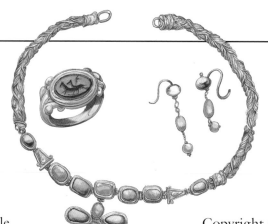

Author: Philip Steele
Editor: Jayne Miller
Designer: John Jamieson
Art editor: Martin Aggett
Art director: Terry Woodley
Picture research: Image Select International
Illustration: Kevin Maddison, Julian Baker, and
Danny McBride

Silver Dolphin Books
An imprint of the Advantage Publishers Group
5880 Oberlin Drive
San Diego, CA 92121-4794
www.advantagebooksonline.com

ISBN 1-57145-553-1

Printed in China.

1 2 3 4 5 02 03 04 05 06

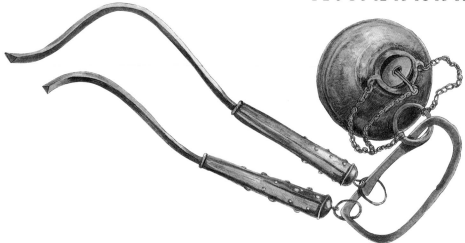

CONTENTS

ROME AND ITS PEOPLE

Rome, the capital of Italy, is a busy, modern city. At its heart, impressive ancient ruins rise above the noisy traffic and crowds. They date back to the age when Rome was at the center of a vast empire. Roman armies battled their way across Europe, Western Asia, and North Africa. After them came peace, trade, and a firm legal system. New roads were built. Fine towns and cities rose up with markets, temples, public baths, and theaters. The Romans created one of the greatest civilizations of the ancient world. It still influences the way we live today, while Latin, the language spoken by the Romans, is the basis of many European languages.

THE POWER OF THE COLOSSEUM

The Colosseum was a massive amphitheater in the middle of Rome, forming an oval 1,739 feet around and four stories high. It first opened its gates to the public in A.D. 80. Imagine the noise as thousands of Romans hurried to the show, buying hot pies from stalls, and clutching their entrance tokens. They would roar as gladiators fought to the death in the arena or were torn apart by wild animals. The Romans may have been civilized, but they were savage, too.

EARLY INDEPENDENCE

According to legend, Rome was founded in 753 B.C. Over the ages it grew from a small farming settlement into a huge city. In 509 B.C., the Romans overthrew their rulers, the *Etruscans* (another group of Mediterranean people). The Romans then formed an independent *republic*, a form of government where representatives are elected to rule.

CONSULS AND TRIBUNES

The city was now governed by an assembly called the *Senate*, whose members belonged to Rome's wealthiest and most powerful families. Each year, the Senate elected two leaders, called consuls. After 493 B.C. the Senate also chose officers called tribunes to look after the interests of ordinary people. During the early period of the Republic, Romans prided themselves on a strict sense of honor and duty.

THE AGE OF EMPIRE

When there was a national crisis, such as during a war, the Senate handed over control to just one person, called a *dictator*. In 49 B.C., a Roman general named Gaius Julius Caesar was declared dictator for life. This marked the end of republican ideals, where the people felt they had some control. By 27 B.C., Caesar's adopted son, Octavian, had become emperor, taking the name Augustus (meaning "honored"). Augustus and future emperors gained more and more personal power, and consulted the Senate far less often. Emperors would rule in Rome for over 400 years, until the year A.D. 476.

ROME'S FOUNDER
Legend tells how Rome was founded by a mythical god named Romulus. He and his twin brother, Remus, were said to have been suckled by a she-wolf when they were babies.

Orange area shows the extent of the Roman Empire in A.D. 117.

Britannia, Germania, Gaul (and other regions of France), Noricum, Dacia, Hispania (and other regions of Spain), Italia, Illyricum, Corsica, Rome, Macedonia, Asia, Lycia, Cilicia, Syria, Achaea, Cyprus, Creta, Armenia, Mauretania, Mediterranean Sea, Arabia Petrae, Arabia, Africa, Aegyptus (Egypt)

SPREAD OF THE ROMAN EMPIRE
By 250 B.C. the Romans had conquered most of the other peoples living in Italy. Successive emperors extended their rule far beyond their homeland, conquering Greece, Spain, and the great North African city of Carthage. Roman armies marched northward into France, Germany, and Britain, and eastward into Egypt and Syria. By the year A.D. 117, the Empire had reached its greatest extent.

MILITARY MIGHT
A marble column in Rome records the military expeditions of the emperor Trajan, who died in A.D. 117.

THE GREAT CITY

Rome was built beside the River Tiber in central Italy. The city covered low-lying areas of drained marsh as well as areas of higher ground known as "the seven hills of Rome," even though most of the hills were less than a hundred feet high. Rome started off as a village of thatched huts and expanded into a great city. It outgrew its walls many times, and by A.D. 90, Rome was home to over a million people.

RUINS OF ROME
The remains of ancient buildings still stand in the city today. These ruins are all that is left of the buildings that surrounded the Forum of Trajan, in ancient Rome.

WELCOME TO ROME

Ancient Rome stood about seventeen miles from Ostia, its port at the mouth of the River Tiber. A network of busy roads converged on the capital, passing tombs and cemeteries on the outskirts of town. It was a sprawling city that teemed with life. First-time visitors to ancient Rome were awed by its magnificent buildings, arches, marble columns, statues, parks, and gardens.

TEMPLES TO THE GODS
This arch was part of a temple built in honor of Faustina, wife of the emperor Antoninus Pius. After her death, in A.D. 141, she was honored as a goddess. The temple stood at the entrance to the old city center, the Forum Romanum, and was built by her husband. It was later made into a Christian church.

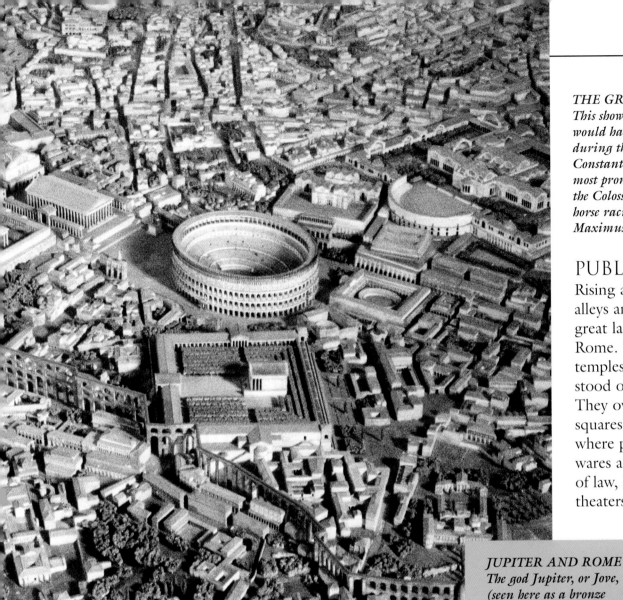

THE GREAT CITY OF ROME
This shows central Rome as it would have appeared in A.D. 320, during the reign of the emperor Constantine the Great. The two most prominent landmarks are the Colosseum (right) and the horse racing circuit of the Circus Maximus (bottom left).

PUBLIC PLACES

Rising above the maze of alleys and backstreets were the great landmarks of ancient Rome. The most ancient temples to the Roman gods stood on the Capitoline Hill. They overlooked *fora* (public squares and shopping centers where people met to sell their wares and do business), courts of law, libraries, racecourses, theaters, and public baths.

JUPITER AND ROME
The god Jupiter, or Jove, (seen here as a bronze statue) was the father of the gods and the protector of the city of Rome. His chief temple was on Rome's Capitoline Hill, but he was worshiped all over the Empire.

LIFE ON THE BLOCK

A visitor to the capital would see few of the low-rise, spacious houses found in smaller towns. In crowded Rome, only the very wealthy could afford a private home, or *domus*, with its own courtyards and water. Most city-dwellers lived in apartment blocks called *insulae* (islands), which could be three to six stories high. The more expensive blocks were residential and offered more privacy. The poorer blocks had workshops, stores, or bars on the ground floor and opened their shutters directly onto noisy streets. The poorer insulae were shoddily built and often caught fire. They did not have a water supply, proper kitchens, or toilets.

CITIZENS AND SLAVES

Over the ages, Rome developed from a republic into an empire, from a small Italian state into a vast and impressive nation governing many different peoples. For most of its history, however, Roman society was always strictly divided according to social class and wealth. Many of the people living in Rome were not rated as citizens at all—they were merely slaves.

A DOG'S LIFE
This disc was chained around the neck of a slave, like a dog's tag. It states the owner's name and asks for the finder to return the slave, should he escape.

TOO MUCH POWER
Huge political powers were handed over to successful general Julius Caesar (100–44 B.C.). Republicans feared he would become king and murdered him.

MEN OF MONEY
The Roman Empire existed to make money, through taxation as well as the import and export of goods. This stone carving shows money changers going about their business. They met at the forum, the financial center of every Roman town.

POWER TO GOVERN

Rome was governed by an assembly called the *Senate*. Its leaders were called consuls. In the early days of the Republic, only members of Rome's oldest and noblest families (the *patricians*) gained positions of power. Later, officials called "tribunes of the people" were elected by the Senate to make sure that the interests of ordinary people (the *plebeians*) were protected. The army was also very powerful, and generals who were successful in military campaigns often turned to politics. After the emperors came to rule Rome, they took most of the Senate's powers for themselves.

SLAVES AND FREEDOM
Roman civilization depended on slave labor. Slaves could be bought and sold all over the Empire. Many of them were prisoners of war captured by the Roman army. Some worked on public building sites or as farm laborers on country estates. Some were forced to toil in the mines, row ships, or fight in the arena as gladiators. Others worked in the home as servants and well-educated Greek slaves were valued as teachers and tutors. Often only the skilled slaves were treated and fed well. Faithful slaves could be granted their freedom after a long service.

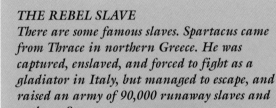
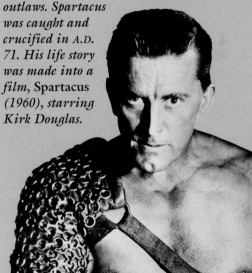

THE REBEL SLAVE
There are some famous slaves. Spartacus came from Thrace in northern Greece. He was captured, enslaved, and forced to fight as a gladiator in Italy, but managed to escape, and raised an army of 90,000 runaway slaves and outlaws. Spartacus was caught and crucified in A.D. 71. His life story was made into a film, Spartacus (1960), starring Kirk Douglas.

THE SERVANT
Found in the ruined Italian town of Pompeii, this painting shows a female domestic slave carrying a plate of cakes. Servants carried out all the everyday tasks in a noble household, from the cooking and cleaning, to childcare and serving the meals.

THE SOCIAL SCALE
Under the emperors, nobility was strictly graded. To be a member of the Senate, a noble needed to be in the topmost rank and be very wealthy. Nobles received favorable treatment in the law courts. Ordinary Romans had few privileges, but even emperors found it difficult to rule if they did not have the support of the public. People from the conquered parts of the Empire were not classed as Roman citizens.

13

EMPERORS OF ROME

As one gladiator pinned down another in the arena of the Colosseum, he would turn to the box where the emperor gazed down on the bloody spectacle. One gesture from the great man, the "thumbs down," and the defeated gladiator would be killed. Such was the power of Rome's emperors. Some rulers were hated by the public; others won lasting respect and admiration.

I POPOLI SARANNO FELICI QVANDO   AVRANNO DEI FILOSOFI PER RE

MARCUS AURELIUS *(A.D. 121–180)*
He was one of the best Roman emperors and an able military leader, but Aurelius is better remembered as a writer, philosopher, and lawmaker.

THE ROAD TO POWER

When Octavian (Augustus) became emperor in 27 B.C. he was careful to call himself *Princeps* or "first citizen." It sounded more democratic, even if his personal powers were becoming greater year by year. His descendants had few such scruples. Early emperors such as Tiberius, Claudius, and Nero were declared gods on their deaths, and the emperor Caligula actually thought he was a god. These were all members of Rome's first imperial family, but later some emperors were put into power by the army. They included Vespasian (A.D. 9–79) and Hadrian (A.D. 76–138).

PLEASING THE CROWD
Roman emperors were as desperate to please the public as modern politicians. They declared public holidays. They gave away free food. They built new venues for chariot racing and combat with gladiators, staging spectacular and often brutal shows. The crowds loved being entertained.

KEEPERS OF THE PEACE

Augustus was a clever and effective ruler. His reign brought the Empire long years of stability known as the *Pax Romana* ("Roman peace"). Other emperors also left their mark. Trajan (A.D. 53–117) was a great administrator and builder and used public funds to help the needy. Hadrian, too, was a wise and able ruler who reorganized the army and supported the arts by funding writers and sculptors.

THE PALACE AT TIVOLI
Between A.D. 124 and 133, the emperor Hadrian built a luxurious country home at Tibur (modern Tivoli), seventeen miles east of Rome. It included libraries, splendid dining halls, baths, gardens, pools decorated with stone crocodiles, and statues by the best Greek sculptors.

THE MAD AND THE BAD

Roman emperors could trust nobody. Plotters, traitors, and poisoners surrounded them. Some were vain, extravagant, and cruel. Caligula (A.D. 12–41) is believed to have become insane. He had many people executed for their money and property, and also murdered his relatives. He forced all inhabitants of the Empire to worship him as a living god, and even made his horse a senator.

Caligula

Nero (A.D. 37–68) was another tyrant who murdered his own relatives. When, in A.D. 64, a dreadful fire raged through Rome, destroying two-thirds of the city, Nero blamed the Christians, a new religious group. He had many of them cruelly put to death. Nero rebuilt Rome (with a splendid palace for himself), but the army rose against him and he committed suicide.

Nero

15

THE ROMAN ARMY

The key to Roman power was its powerful army. In the early days of the republic, any male from a land-owning family between seventeen and forty-six years old could be called up to serve his country. Commanders picked the fittest and strongest men among them for each campaign. In 107 B.C. the great general Gaius Marius (157–86 B.C.) created a new, full-time army, which any citizen could join. This was the army that created the Roman Empire.

Roman officer

Praetorian guard

Infantry

JOINING THE LEGION

Roman armies tramped the length and breadth of Europe. They were the most disciplined troops the world had ever seen, making up a deadly fighting machine that could conquer and control an empire. The early imperial army was organized into twenty-eight sections called legions. Each of these had about 5,500 men. Their battle standard was an eagle of gold. Non-legionary support troops were called auxiliaries. These included cavalry, specialist forces, and recruits from distant parts of the Empire. Non-Roman citizens were allowed to join the auxiliaries.

TORTOISE FORMATION
When Roman soldiers were storming a fort, they often formed a "tortoise." They crouched behind their shields, turning them outward or upward, rim to rim, to form a kind of shell. Stones, spears, and arrows bounced off this as the soldiers edged forward.

A SOLDIER'S LIFE

Each legionary carried a sword, a shield, and a pole over his shoulder, which clanked with pots, pans, and digging tools. The legionaries were not just fighters but builders and engineers. Soldiers built the roads, bridges, and forts needed to help them invade, conquer, and defend new lands. Marching rations were basic— a hard biscuit, bacon, cheese, and salt. A soldier would serve for twenty-five years, and would then normally retire to settle down and marry. Non-Roman auxiliaries who served for twenty-five years were given Roman citizenship.

Standard bearer

Auxiliary infantry

Legionary on the march

UNITED WE STAND
Trajan's column in Rome shows troops conquering lands around the River Danube (A.D. 101–106).

A FINE SWORD
This sword and scabbard were found at Mainz, in Germany. They were made in about 15 B.C. Roman swords at this time were short and deadly. Decorations on the scabbard show Augustus with his stepson Tiberius, who fought with the army in campaigns all over Europe.

VICTORY AND DEFEAT

Brave soldiers were rewarded with riches or trophies, while a general who had completed a major conquest was awarded a "triumph"— a splendid victory procession through the city of Rome. This honor was later taken over by the reigning emperor who was keen to take the credit for any victory. Defeats were not unknown. In A.D. 9, three entire legions were wiped out in a single battle in Germany.

17

FRONTIER FORTS

To people living on the edges of the Empire, the city of Rome was a distant dream. The only Rome they knew was the local army fort, but this often offered a scaled-down version of life in a Roman city.

DEFENDING THE EMPIRE

Conquered lands had to be protected. Permanent forts, built from local timber, or from stone and turf, soon replaced temporary army camps. Roman forts had watchtowers, a command headquarters, soldiers' barracks, parade grounds, granaries for storing food, toilets, and public baths. Near some forts there were temples and even amphitheaters—miniature copies of the Colosseum, with gladiator shows to entertain the troops. Towns often grew up around the forts, which became thriving centers of trade, with law courts and tax offices. Many retired soldiers set up homes in the towns. The native people were encouraged to intermarry with Roman soldiers and their families, and adopt the Roman style of life. This secured Rome's control of its empire just as much as military power.

SKILLED SOLDIERS
Roman soldiers carried all the tools necessary for setting up camp, digging defenses, and building forts. While on the march, their packs might weigh as much as sixty-six pounds.

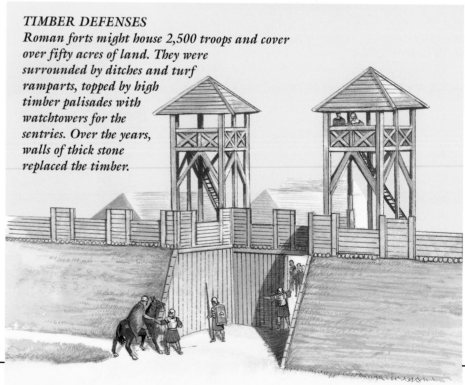

TIMBER DEFENSES
Roman forts might house 2,500 troops and cover over fifty acres of land. They were surrounded by ditches and turf ramparts, topped by high timber palisades with watchtowers for the sentries. Over the years, walls of thick stone replaced the timber.

ALONG THE WALL

The weakest sections of the Roman frontier were protected by long defensive walls. One, called the Limes, ran for 344 miles along the Rhine and Danube rivers. Another, Hadrian's Wall, ran across northern Britain between the River Tyne and the Solway Firth, a distance of seventy-five miles. It linked together sixteen major forts, each garrisoned by about 1,000 troops, as well as smaller forts, holding units of about a hundred soldiers.

HADRIAN'S WALL

Hadrian's Wall was built between A.D. 122 and 126. Its purpose was to repel attacks by tribes from the north and to control their movement. It also provided a safe route for communications and trade.

GRAIN STORE
Every Roman fort had a granary (or grain store), built of timber or stone. The floor was raised on pillars, which are all that have survived from the Roman fort granary pictured above. The pillars kept the grain dry and free from vermin.

FORT OF THE SAXON SHORE
The Romans built stone forts, similar to the castles of the Middle Ages, to defend southeast Britain from attack by fierce Saxon warriors from Germany.

FORTRESS LIFE

An officer's life on the empire's frontier forts, whether in Africa, Asia, or Europe, could be pleasant enough. In times of peace he could hold dinner parties, go hunting, or write letters. For legionaries and auxiliaries, the routine was dull. The days were spent drilling on the parade-ground, marching, or playing dice. At some forts there was a bathhouse for use by the whole regiment. In times of war or uprising, frontier life was dangerous. Enemy arrows could set the fort on fire and patrols could be ambushed and massacred.

ROADS AND TRANSPORT

When the Colosseum was being built, the Romans thought nothing of building a broad, new road to transport stone from the Albulae quarries (near modern Tivoli). Roman road-building was not bettered in Europe until the 1800s, and many modern roads are based on the old Roman routes.

ACROSS THE EMPIRE

The Roman Empire extended about 2,500 miles from east to west and 2,315 miles from north to south. This vast area was crisscrossed by a network of roads, which were long, straight, and paved with closely-fitting flagstones. Roads made it possible for armies to move quickly from one trouble spot to another. Official messengers could ride at speed on the roads, picking up new horses from stables along the route.

a groma was used to check right angles

tightly packed flagstones

timber supports

layer of gravel

layers of stones and chippings

MARKING THE MILES
A Roman mile was based on a thousand paces, which was 1,620 yards. Road distances were carved or painted on milestones placed at regular intervals along the highway. Local governors were responsible for putting up accurate milestones and repairing the roads, not the Senate in Rome.

TRAVELING THE ROADS

The quickest way to travel along the roads of the Empire was by horseback or mule. Mules were also used to pull light, two-wheel or four-wheel passenger carts. Heavy loads, such as supplies brought in by ship to the seaports, were carried on rumbling wagons, hauled by two powerful oxen.

ROAD BUILDING
Roman roads were carefully surveyed and measured out. A typical road would be bedded down with layers of local gravel and stones. Over boggy ground, heavy timber piles would support the roadway.

ITY STREETS

ty streets were also surfaced in stone.
ey were bordered by curbs and by raised
vements covered with chips of brick set in
ortar. Streets had gutters, but must have
en very muddy, because stepping stones
re provided in places. Traffic jams and
ise were a common problem even then.
entually, wagons were banned from streets
ring the day, but this made the nights
ry noisy for people trying to get to sleep.

PATHS OF POMPEII
*In A.D. 79 the town of Pompeii in
southwest Italy was buried when the
volcano Vesuvius erupted. Its ancient
streets have since been excavated by
archaeologists. We now know that
Pompeii's streets were surfaced with
hard blocks of volcanic rock. Streets
varied in width from eight to
twenty-three feet.*

THE ROAD TO ROME
*Shipments of grain from North Africa, wine from
southern Gaul (France), or wool from Britain would
have been landed at the
seaport of Ostia and then
carried by cart to the
capital along this road.*

DAILY LIFE IN ANCIENT ROME

HOME AND FAMILY

The family was at the heart of Roman society. A family unit included aunts, uncles, cousins, and grandparents, who often lived together or close by. A man usually had authority over his wife and children, as well as over the household slaves. He was normally responsible for earning a living, while his wife managed the day-to-day running of the household. However, we do know that some women also ran successful businesses and often played an important part in town affairs.

A ROMAN WEDDING

Roman girls were engaged to be married at twelve, and boys at fourteen, although the wedding took place some years later. A sum of money, the dowry, was paid by the bride's family. In return, the bridegroom gave gifts and a wedding ring to the bride. A sheep or a pig was sacrificed to the gods, to mark the ceremony and wedding vows were exchanged.

PUBLIC BATHS
Going to the baths was a regular activity for all family members—although not together. Bathing was a form of entertainment and a meeting place, as much as a way to get clean.

PROTECTING THE HOME

In every Roman house was a small wooden shrine, or *larium*, a cabinet containing little statues of gods who were believed to look after the family and the home. The family would make offerings of wine, honey or cakes at the shrine every day. Household gods were called *Penates*. The hearth was regarded as sacred to the Penates, and a flame was always kept alight in their honor. The table was also a sacred place, and most families set a bowl of fruit and salt ready for the gods. One of the Penates, or household gods, was called the Lar. He represented the spirit of the family's ancestors. He also made sure that the family would not suffer from hunger or hardship.

THE LAR
*This Lar holds a horn
called a cornucopia in
his left hand, a symbol
of plenty. In his right
hand is a rhyton, or
drinking cup.*

The bride wore a white tunic, a saffron-colored cloak, and sandals. A veil of bright orange covered her eyes and she wore a wreath of marjoram, verbena, or orange blossom in her hair. That evening, a torch-lit procession led the couple to their new home. This was likely to have been rooms within a parent's large home, unless they were wealthy, or—for the majority of the population—a rented apartment in a tenement block.

CHILDREN AT HOME

In Republican Rome, children were treated with strict discipline. In the days of the Empire, however, it became normal for parents to show children much more affection. The children of the wealthier families were mostly looked after by the household slaves, whom they often knew better than their parents.

ELEGANT FURNISHINGS
*Wealthy Romans slept
on comfortable beds,
and had elaborate
furniture, such as
wooden stools, chairs,
chests and couches.
Lighting was provided
by oil lamps or candles.*

FASHION AND STYLE

For most working Romans, everyday costume was a simple wool tunic or shift. For the middle and upper classes, getting dressed was a more complicated matter, requiring the help of slaves. Men draped themselves in a bulky white, linen robe called a toga. *Women wore a long dress, called a* stola, *as well as a shawl (or* palla) *which could be draped over the head and shoulders. Although soldiers wore breeches and farmers would often bind their legs with strips of cloth, most Romans believed that only barbarians, such as Celts or Asians, wore trousers.*

THE COLOR OF MONEY

In ancient Rome, cloth could be dyed in many colors. Dyes were often made from plants such as madder (for red), woad (for blue), and crocus (for yellow). Unmarried girls always wore white clothes. The color purple was reserved for the emperor himself. However, boys from noble families wore a robe or toga with a narrow purple edge, and senators had a broad purple band on their togas as a badge of their high office. Purple dye was made from shellfish.

CRAFTED JEWELS
Roman goldsmiths were skilled craftsmen who produced bands of metal or delicate twists of gold wire. These have colored glass beads set in them.

WRAPS AND DRAPES
Clothes like this were being worn by members of Rome's imperial family about 2,000 years ago. The mother wears a stola and palla, while her young son already wears a toga.

STRAPPED UP
Most Romans wore leather sandals, similar to the ones shown here, or a tougher nail-studded version. Shoes and laced slippers were also worn, while army officers often wore boots.

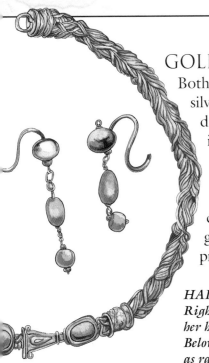

GOLD AND GLITTER

Both men and women wore rings of gold, silver, or bronze on their fingers, often decorated with portraits, patterns, or inscriptions. Women wore bangles, bracelets, earrings, and sometimes several necklaces at once, while ornate pins and brooches were used to fasten clothes. Jewelry was often set with real gems, including pearls, amber, jet, and precious stones from all over the Empire.

HAIRY MOMENTS
Right: A domestic slave helps her mistress to pin up her hair in the latest style.
Below: In ancient Europe, fashions did not change as rapidly as they do today. Even so, hairstyles for both men and women did vary greatly over the ages.

HAIR AND MAKEUP

Hairstyles, created with combs and hairpins of ivory, reflected changing fashions, often set by the Emperor's wife and family. Ladies might wear their hair curled, in a bun, or tucked under a headdress. Wigs and hair extensions were popular accessories. Perfume and oils were stored in beautiful little flasks and cosmetics were available, including all sorts of powders, paints, lipstick, and eyeshadow—some of which were actually poisonous.

DINING IN ANCIENT ROME

Nearly 2,000 years ago, a Roman nobleman named Marcus Gavius Apicius wrote down a list of his favorite recipes. These included tripe in honey and ginger, nettle quiche, and a custard made of rose hips and calf's brains. That was not typical of the daily Roman diet. Most Romans ate far simpler foods, but banquets and feasts were a feature of imperial Rome.

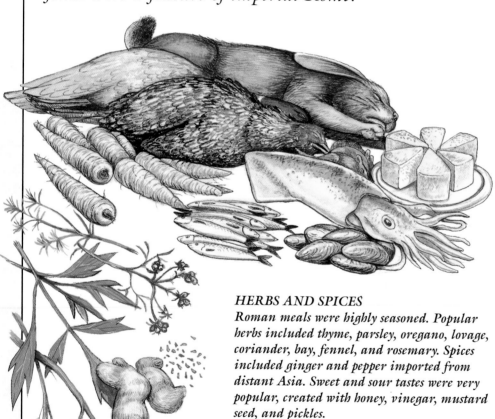

HERBS AND SPICES
Roman meals were highly seasoned. Popular herbs included thyme, parsley, oregano, lovage, coriander, bay, fennel, and rosemary. Spices included ginger and pepper imported from distant Asia. Sweet and sour tastes were very popular, created with honey, vinegar, mustard seed, and pickles.

COOKS' TOOLS
Roman kitchens were small and smoky. Brick-built, wood-fired stoves were used for boiling vegetables and stews or grilling meat. They were filled with saucepans, tins, and cauldrons (large pots) for cooking, plus sieves, ladles, knives, and large pottery storage jars.

glass jug

pan

strainer

mortar

baking tin

pestle

PREPARING FOOD
A Roman breakfast was a light snack, perhaps a crust of bread with some olives. Lunch also needed little preparation—boiled eggs, bacon or sausage, and a bowl of figs. During the afternoon, slaves would bring buckets of water and start a fire in the brick stove. The cook would grind herbs and spices with a pestle and mortar, or begin ladling out a tangy fish sauce while dinner was being prepared.

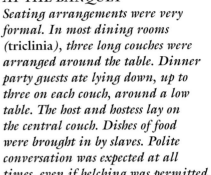

AT THE BANQUET

Seating arrangements were very formal. In most dining rooms (triclinia), three long couches were arranged around the table. Dinner party guests ate lying down, up to three on each couch, around a low table. The host and hostess lay on the central couch. Dishes of food were brought in by slaves. Polite conversation was expected at all times, even if belching was permitted.

FAST FOOD

Small city bars called thermopolia served watered-down wine, as well as food from large, covered jars which were set into the counter. Lunchtime snacks included stews, soups, beans, salads, sausages, fried fish, and Roman versions of pizza and pasta. This is the remains of one such fast-food outlet in Ostia.

POVERTY AND GREED

A few very rich Romans liked to throw lavish dinner parties, or banquets. Gourmet dishes might include elaborate pies, honey-roast dormice with poppy seeds, peacock eggs, or snails. Some guests ate until they were sick—and then started all over again. Many Romans disapproved of such greed. Poor Romans had a starchy diet, mostly of bread or grain mixed with water, rather like porridge or the polenta eaten in Italy today. People who could afford better food dined off pork, chicken, or goose with peas, beans, or leeks. Meals were washed down with diluted wine.

AT THE BATHS

In the later days of the Empire, the city of Rome had over 800 thermae or public baths. Baths founded by the Romans are still to be seen all over Europe, as are towns named after Roman baths, from Bath in England to Baden-Baden in Germany.

STEAM AND TOWELS

Public baths were often magnificent buildings with under-floor heating. Currents of hot air from furnaces were directed under raised floors. The largest baths had cold plunges, warm rooms, hot rooms, saunas, individual tubs, shallow pools, swimming pools, changing rooms, and exercise halls. Men and women normally bathed in separate areas, or at different times of the day. For many, the best part of the visit was a rub-down with oil followed by a massage. They would emerge clean and relaxed.

BATHING AT BATH
*Warm, healing springs at Bath in southern Britain were welled up from underground, pumping out a quarter of a million gallons of water every day. The waters were sacred to the British Celts who lived there and also to the Roman invaders. The Romans called the site **Aquae Sulis** and built a temple, a town, and public baths, which may still be seen.*

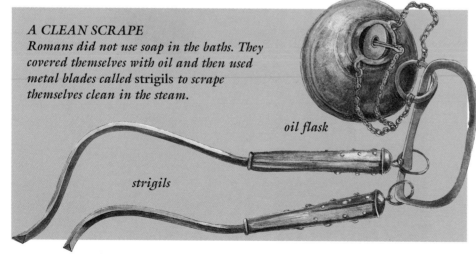

A CLEAN SCRAPE
*Romans did not use soap in the baths. They covered themselves with oil and then used metal blades called **strigils** to scrape themselves clean in the steam.*

oil flask

strigils

ROMAN PLUMBING

The Romans were first-rate plumbers. Our world "plumbing" comes from *plumbum*, the Roman word for lead. Lead pipes and tanks were all part of the main water system that connected public baths and the houses of the wealthy with the aqueducts that brought water into the towns. Even in distant parts of the Empire, Roman engineers built massive drains and sewers beneath their towns to carry away waste. These were lined with stone or timber.

COMMUNAL BATHROOM
Public toilets were often located at the bath house where waste water from the baths could be used to flush away sewage along a channel. The toilet seats were made of stone or wood and were arranged in rows without doors or partitions. Sponges on sticks were used instead of toilet tissue.

PASSING THE TIME

Going to the baths offered men and women a chance to meet up with friends, to discuss business or politics, or just to relax and chat. The more energetic young Romans would work out with athletic exercises or ball games. The lazier ones might throw dice.

BATH TIME
Bathing was an important part of everyday life for the Romans and featured in many many works of art. This picture shows spirits or nymphs bathing as if they were at the public baths.

LETTERS AND LEARNING

The ancient Romans spoke a language called Latin. Many of the languages spoken in Europe today have their origins in Latin, including Italian, Spanish, Romanian, and French. English words that have come from Latin include "letter" and "literature" from littera.

INSCRIPTION (right)
Latin was originally written only in separate capital letters, but in the later years of the Empire, joined-up handwriting and lowercase letters began to be used.

LETTERS AND NUMBERS

The letters used in English and in many other modern languages are based on the Roman alphabet. The Roman script was developed from that of the ancient *Etruscans*. The Romans used a different set of numerals, although they are still sometimes used today. They are based on the figures I (1), V (5), X (10), L (50), C (100), D (500), and M (1,000). So eleven was written as "XI" and forty as "XL."

LEARNING TO READ
This painting from Pompeii illustrated the importance of learning. It shows the Greek god Dionysus learning to read as a boy. He recites from a scroll of parchment while his mother waits to hand him another. Greek culture was a great influence on the Romans.

TAKE A NOTE
Romans could write with pen and ink on parchment (animal hide) or on papyrus (paper made from reeds). A point, called a stylus, was also used to scratch notes into a waxed tablet.

parchment

ink

pen

stylus

wax tablet

LIBRARIES
Famous writers would recite their poetry or their histories to groups of friends. Those not invited could buy handwritten copies of the works from book shops or read them at public libraries. Emperors and wealthy people had their own private libraries such as the one below.

GOING TO SCHOOL
The Roman Empire needed educated citizens, such as engineers who understood measurements and soldiers who could keep accounts. There were some basic schools which taught boys and girls reading, writing, and mathematics. The teaching was dull and pupils were beaten regularly. Wealthy boys and some girls had private tutors. As these pupils grew older, they learned how to speak in public and studied poetry and history.

GREEK CONNECTIONS
The Romans were great admirers of the Greek arts. Young Romans from noble families were expected to learn the Greek language. Romans read and imitated Greek writers and even adopted Greek gods. The light comedies of the Greek playwright Menander (c. 343–291 B.C.), below, were the most popular in ancient Rome.

WRITERS AND THINKERS
Ancient Rome produced many great lawyers, thinkers, and writers. The poet Virgil (70–19 B.C.) wrote about the adventures of Aeneas, a prince from Troy who, according to a legend, traveled to Italy and founded Rome. Ovid (43 B.C.–A.D. 17) wrote fine love poetry. However, in A.D. 8 he offended the authorities, and the emperor Augustus banished him to the Black Sea, on the edges of the Empire. A writer's success could depend on approval from the emperor.

COUNTRY LIFE

The Roman poet Virgil was born and raised on a farm. He disliked the politics and the bustle of the capital and preferred to write about everyday life in the countryside, which gives historians a glimpse of Roman country life. However, even here there were great social differences between the wealthy villa owner and the lowly farmer.

VILLAS AND ESTATES

Grand country houses were called villas. They were large buildings with magnificent rooms, gardens, courtyards, private baths, and even central heating. The emperors' villas, built in the Italian countryside, were vast luxurious palaces. Villas were built all over the Roman Empire. Most were surrounded by large, farmed estates with orchards of fruit trees and fields of crops tended by slaves. In warmer lands there were vineyards and olive groves. North African estates produced essential wheat, while in northern Europe, sheep were raised to supply wool and apples were grown.

AN IMPERIAL VILLA
The country villa of the emperor Hadrian (below) provided him with a haven from the troubles of political life, with peaceful gardens, pools, and marble columns.

VILLA ARCHITECTURE
The grandest villas could be seen in the Italian countryside and beside the Mediterranean Sea. Their architecture was imitated elsewhere. All over the Empire, governors and local rulers built themselves villas with covered walkways and gardens, although usually on a smaller scale.

TOILING IN THE TILES
In this mosaic, a laborer works his team of oxen. Roman farms varied from small holdings of about an acre to huge estates of several thousand acres. Wheat, rye, barley, and oats were generally sown, reaped, and threshed by hand.

SMALL FARMS

When a Roman soldier retired from the army, he could take a grant of land instead of a pension. Many veterans set up small holdings, raising geese and pigs, growing vegetables, and keeping bees. In distant parts of the Empire, local tribes still farmed the land for a living, giving part of their produce to the Romans as a form of tax.

BEE KEEPING
Farms of all sizes kept hives of bees. The Romans did not use sugar, so honey was the only sweetener used in the preparation and cooking of food.

WORKING ON THE LAND

A farm laborer's life was one of endless toil. There were few machines to make work easier, although a reaper was invented in Gaul (Roman France). Oxen were trained to haul heavy farm wagons and simple plows, while sheep's wool was clipped with iron shears. Farmers knew how to irrigate and drain the land and had some knowledge of soils and selecting crops which were most suitable. Like farmers today, they enriched their fields with manure and compost.

OX POWER
A team of oxen strain against the yoke on a modern Italian farm, a scene that has changed little in 2,000 years. Farmers in ancient Rome would often yoke boisterous young oxen together with older, gentler creatures in order to train them for field work. There were no machines to help.

MONEY AND TRADE

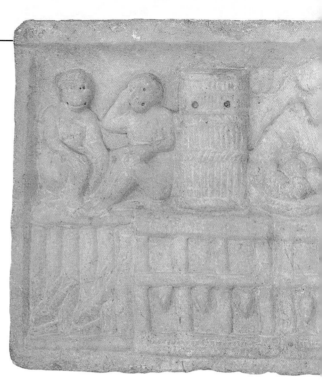

The earliest Romans exchanged goods rather than using money to buy things. Under this system of barter, one ox was worth ten sheep. When money was introduced, it was still called pecunia, *which came from the Latin word* pecus, *meaning "livestock." By 280 B.C. the Romans had copied the Greeks in minting metal coins. Silver coinage was first issued in 269 B.C., and when Rome gained control of rich mines in Spain, it became the financial capital of the world. Later in the Empire, however, the economy weakened—which meant that prices of goods rose sharply and Roman coins were devalued.*

ROMAN COINS
Mints were set up all over the Empire and coins were stamped with the emperor's head on one side, and also with emblems of the Empire's might, such as ships and horseback soldiers.

CONTAINER TRADE
Liquids such as olive oil or wine were often transported in tall pottery jars called amphorae. Full amphorae have survived in many Roman shipwrecks discovered around the Mediterranean Sea, the Black Sea, and along the coasts of northern Europe. Historians have also been able to trace trading connections through pottery pieces discovered around the Empire. Other goods, such as grain, were transported in sacks, bales, or barrels.

DOING BUSINESS

Each major Roman town had a *forum* or business center. Rome itself had several. Here were law courts, town council buildings, headquarters of craftworkers' guilds, shops, and market stalls. Shoppers in ancient Rome were greeted by the shouts of traders advertising their wares—loaves of bread, joints of meat, fish, olive oil, pots and pans, lamps, precious glass bottles, sandals, and boots. Trading officials roamed the forum to see that people were not cheated.

ROMAN WORKSHOPS

Many craft goods were produced in small workshops or in studios behind the shop. Others were mass-produced in what were considered the first factories. A single pottery in Gaul or Germany would turn out dishes and bowls for export by the thousand, each stamped with the manufacturer's trademark.

"COME AND BUY!"
An everyday Roman market scene is preserved in this stone carving. An apple is bought from a street stall on market day. Many towns also had permanent covered market halls.

ROMAN RICHES
Roman coins were kept in chests, money-boxes, and purses. In times of trouble, hoards of coins were often buried in secret places for safety. Hoards, such as this one below found at a Saxon Shore Fort, are still discovered today in lands which were once part of the Roman Empire.

IMPORTS AND EXPORTS

Business was not just the result of Rome's vast empire. It was the purpose of it. The desire for rich mineral resources, timber, farmland, and building materials spurred Roman rulers on to capture new lands. The expanding empire also provided opportunities for taxation and new markets for Roman goods. Imports and exports were a matter of life and death. About 400,000 tons of grain were shipped into Rome each year, mostly from North Africa. Without these supplies, the people of Rome would have starved.

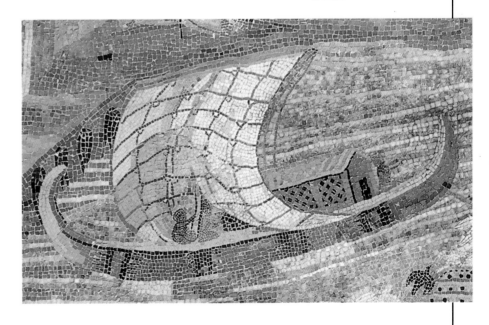

NILE CARGOES
A Roman painting shows a river boat on the River Nile in Egypt. Egypt provided Rome with wheat and cotton.

GODS AND GODDESSES

The Romans worshiped many different gods and goddesses. The two-faced Janus was the father of all their gods, and was honored in the name of the month "January." He was also thought to guard doorways, as he could look both ways at once. Jupiter or Jove was the protector of the state—he was the sky god who hurled thunderbolts when angered. Mars was the god of war. Juno was the moon-goddess who cared for childbirth, while Vesta was the goddess of fire and her spirit was thought to protect the family hearth. Ceres was the goddess of corn. Her name is remembered today when we eat "cereal" for breakfast.

MINERVA (left)
Wise Minerva was the Roman goddess of war and peace, and protected arts and crafts. She is one of the "Capitoline triad," along with Jupiter and Juno, as all three had shrines on Capitoline Hill.

SERAPIS (right)
Serapis and Isis were the Egyptian god and goddess of fertility. In the A.D. 200s they became popular with Romans throughout the Empire, and were worshiped as far north as Britain.

TEMPLES AND FESTIVALS

Magnificent temples were raised all over the Roman Empire. These were built to honor the gods, rather than as places of public worship. Romans did not attend temples regularly, instead they left offerings at shrines or prayed to the gods for particular favors. There were many religious festivals. Each December, there were wild celebrations for Saturnalia (which honored the god Saturn). Servants would exchange places with their masters for a day, and families would exchange gifts. The Roman emperor acted as high priest, sacrificing animals to the gods for important festivals and state occasions.

LOOKING FOR SIGNS

Romans were very superstitious. The left side was considered unlucky—the word "sinister" comes from the Latin word for left, and Augustus is said to have always put on his right shoe first. Romans believed there were unlucky days, and on these, the Senate would not meet or work. The Senate would consult *augurs* to decide the best dates to invade, or on which to hold an event. Augurs were officials who looked out for signs from the gods, which they would detect in flashes of lightning or the flight of birds.

FOREIGN RELIGIONS

Many beliefs about the Roman gods were shared with those of the Greeks. Jupiter was the Roman version of the Greek Zeus, Mars was the same as the Greek war god Ares, and Minerva was linked to Greek goddess Athene. Romans readily adopted religions from Egypt and other parts of the Empire. Mithras, the Persian sun god, was a favorite with the legions. Temples to Mithras, where bulls were sacrificed, were built at many forts. The Romans' openness to other religions helped Christianity to spread quickly through the provinces, once it was allowed (see page 50). It was firmly rooted by A.D. 200.

STONY GAZE
Medusa was a monster from Greek mythology, adopted by the Romans. According to legend, one look at her could turn you to stone.

MARS
The month of March takes its names from Mars. He was the Roman god of war, and legionaries trained for combat on Rome's Campus Martius ("field of Mars"). His wife was Venus, goddess of love and beauty.

MURALS AND MOSAICS

Roman artists were commissioned to decorate the walls and floors of private houses. They made pictures of gods and goddesses, heroes and heroines, country landscapes, hunting scenes, and still-life paintings. Murals (large wall paintings) were created on mounted wooden panels or as frescoes— scenes painted directly on to the plaster.

ANCIENT ART
Uncovered by excavators in Pompeii, this wall painting has survived for 2,000 years.

LAVISH DECORATIONS (left)
This beautiful fresco, on the wall of a Roman villa, includes painted-on columns and pillars. Such features acted as optical illusions, tricking the eye.

WALL PAINTINGS

Many Roman homes were richly decorated in warm red, green, black, and gold. Roman artists loved bold colors and patterns. They liked to trick the eye by painting false pillars, niches, and marble slabs on the walls. These framed the portraits and landscapes around the room. Many of the paintings were very realistic, although Roman artists had not fully mastered the art of perspective (showing dimensions and spatial difference between objects).

PICTURES IN PIECES

Beautiful mosaics covered the floors of many Roman villas and town houses, baths, and other public buildings. These were pictures made from thousands of small fragments of colored pottery, stone or glass (known as *tesserae*). The pictures of landscapes, gods, and heroes were bordered with elaborate patterns. A good mosaic could be a great work of art, yet smooth to walk on and far more durable than a painting. Many mosaics have survived hundreds of years buried beneath sand or soil before being uncovered by archaeologists.

MOLDED PLASTER

Plaster made from ground stone and chalk is called stucco. The Romans used it to make intricate moldings on their ceilings, walls, and at the top of columns. Sometimes artists worked stucco wall panels into paintings of human figures, landscapes, and buildings to make them three-dimensional.

SCENES FROM
A VILLA (above)
This fine mosaic comes from Tunisia, in North Africa. The artist shows everyday life around a Roman villa, such as farming and hunting.

3-D DESIGN
Temples, horses, and figures have been the inspiration for this stucco decoration from Rome. The style suggests that the artist may have been Egyptian.

MAKING A MOSAIC
Mosaic makers needed to be highly skilled craftspeople as well as artists. They would draw the outline of their design on wet cement first. The colored tesserae were then arranged into pictures and pressed into the cement.

STONE SCULPTURE

The Romans placed marble statues almost everywhere—in their temples, in the forum, and in their own private gardens. Over time, stone has survived when wood and paint have decayed, so today we can see Roman sculpture in all its glory.

STATUES AND RELIEFS

Roman rulers decorated their cities with impressive statues and stone reliefs (three-dimensional panels or friezes). These might show gods or emperors, and sometimes emperors as gods. The Romans were great admirers of Greek sculpture. Like the Greeks, they often idealized the human body, trying to show it at its most perfect. At the end of the republican period, however, Roman sculptors began to make very realistic statues, showing that even leaders have wrinkles and scars.

SOARING STONE
Most Roman temples and public buildings had stone columns, with ornate tops called capitals. *The designs of these were based on styles used in Greece.*

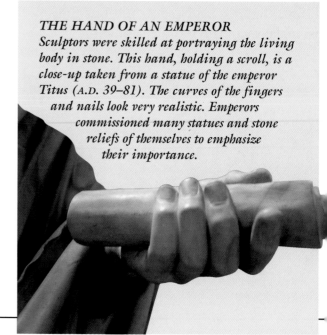

THE HAND OF AN EMPEROR
Sculptors were skilled at portraying the living body in stone. This hand, holding a scroll, is a close-up taken from a statue of the emperor Titus (A.D. 39–81). The curves of the fingers and nails look very realistic. Emperors commissioned many statues and stone reliefs of themselves to emphasize their importance.

HISTORY IN STONE
(above) Powerful images
on monuments, such as
Trajan's Column,
glorified Rome's history.

GOING UP (right)
Inside the hollow marble
drums that make up
Trajan's Column is a
spiral staircase.

STORY OF SOLDIERS

In A.D. 113 a new forum was completed in the city of Rome, built under the instructions of the emperor Trajan. Towering above it was a column 115 feet high. This was faced with twenty-three curved panels unfolding the story of Trajan's military campaigns. Sculptors made the marble come alive with carvings of thousands of individual soldiers.

QUARRYING
Sculptors worked with blocks of marble
found at Carerra in Italy. It is still
quarried there today (above). Marble is a
crystalized form of limestone, which has a
hard surface that can be polished for a smooth
finish. The Romans also got marble from the
Greek island of Paros, and Majorca in Spain.

EVERYDAY IMAGES

Many reliefs, such as those that have survived on tombstones, show scenes of ordinary people leading their daily lives. These give us a fascinating glimpse of how people lived in the days of Rome. We can see Roman children, noble ladies, market traders, butchers, teachers, pupils, doctors, and gladiators. Such memorials have been discovered all over the Empire.

BUILDERS AND ENGINEERS

The Romans were the greatest architects and civil engineers of the ancient world. They invented new building materials and developed architectural structures such as arches and domes. Many of their city walls, bridges, aqueducts, and great public buildings still stand today. Even so, some of their building work was shoddy, notably the capital's high-rise apartment blocks. These were intended for ordinary, working class citizens in Rome. They were built cheaply with mud walls that cracked and were badly ventilated with no heating.

ROMAN ARCHITECTS

The surviving buildings of the Romans astound modern architects. There is the great circular temple to all the gods, the Pantheon, topped by a massive dome. Completed around A.D. 124, this was the largest enclosed space in the world for hundreds of years. Roman engineers raised powerful arches and soaring columns. They overcame extraordinary natural obstacles. For example, the triple-layered aqueduct known as the Pont-du-Gard, in France, rises more than 156 feet from the valley floor.

BUILDING BRICKS
Romans used brick, stone, and concrete to build. Volcanic rock called tufa *was widely used in Italy, while granite and limestone were quarried across the Empire.*

THE GREAT ARENA
This grand amphitheater was built by the Romans at Arles, in southern Gaul, about 1,925 years ago. It held 20,000 spectators and was ringed by sixty arches.

STRONG CONCRETE

By about A.D. 50, Roman builders had made one of the most important inventions in the history of architecture. It was concrete, made with a base of a reddish-colored volcanic sand. The result was a material that was lightweight but very strong. This was the secret of their colossal domes and arches.

HEAVING AND HAULING

How did the Romans manage to raise great buildings without modern machinery, excavators, and bulldozers? They used muscle power. They had a large, free workforce in the form of slaves. Cranes for lifting heavy stone blocks could be powered by wooden treadwheels, turned by the trampling feet of the hard-working slaves.

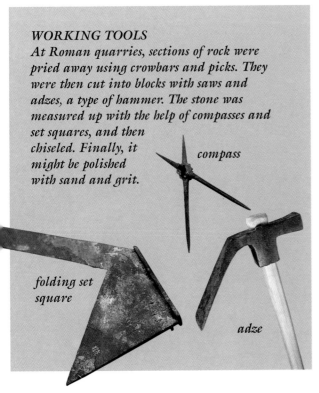

WORKING TOOLS
At Roman quarries, sections of rock were pried away using crowbars and picks. They were then cut into blocks with saws and adzes, a type of hammer. The stone was measured up with the help of compasses and set squares, and then chiseled. Finally, it might be polished with sand and grit.

compass

folding set square

adze

GREAT ARCHES
The aqueduct built at Segovia in Spain is an engineering marvel. It has 128 arches, up to 90 feet high, and was built of blocks of white granite. These were dry-jointed, which means that no mortar or cement was used to bond them together. Its purpose was to bring fresh water from the Frío river into the city.

ENTERTAINING ROMANS

The English word "person" comes from the Latin word persona. *Originally, the persona was the mask worn by an actor in a play, which helped to amplify the sound of the voice. Later, it meant just an actor or member of the cast. Plays—and other entertainment— were very important to Romans.*

ORANGE THEATER
The theater at Orange in southern France is one of the best-preserved from the Roman world. It could hold 9,000 people, seated around thirty-seven tiers.

THEATER-GOING
Theaters were so popular that the Romans built them as far away as Jordan and Libya so that troops and Roman settlers there could enjoy performances. In Rome itself, the Theater of Pompeii (built in 55 B.C.) could seat an audience of 27,000. Actors were respected and treated much as film stars are today. Greek plays such as comedies by the writer Menander were the most popular in Rome. Roman productions concentrated on spectacle, song, and pantomime.

MASKED ACTORS
Roman actors did not go in for method acting; they wore masks on stage—sad ones for a tragic character or grinning ones to show a comic role.

CING FRENZY
*eys performed all
s of daring feats on
seback to entertain
d win support from
crowds. Chariot races
re started by the sound
trumpet and were
, furious, and very
gerous. Twelve
riots at a time could
e on a circuit .*

THE RACES

the age of the
perors, theater took
ond place to chariot
ing as entertainment.
me's main stadium,
Circus Maximus
reat Circus) was 1,980
t long and 660 feet wide, and could hold
5,000 fans. Chariots were normally pulled
teams of four horses, and shows would
include stunts and acrobatics. Top
rioteers, such as a racer named Diocles,
ame famous and wealthy.

MAKING MUSIC

Music was played in the home, but was
less important to the Romans than it
had been to the ancient Greeks. Most
popular was the rousing music that
accompanied military triumphs and
gladiator shows. Percussion came from
cymbals, tambourines,
and rattles. Wind
instruments included
flutes and panpipes.

LITTLE LYRES
*The most common
stringed instruments
were the lyre and the
cithara, which were both
varieties of harp often
played in the home.*

ROMAN GAMES
*Adults and children loved
to play games, with names
such as "tables," "thieves,"
and "three-stones." There
were no boards, just an
outline drawn in the sand
or cement, such as this one.*

AT THE COLOSSEUM

Providing impressive entertainment was one of the most important ways an emperor could win the support of the people and stay popular. Under their rule, public entertainment in Rome became ever more savage and cruel. Plays and chariot racing were overshadowed by gory gladiator shows. Nowhere was torture and bloodshed more terrible than on the arena of the Colosseum in Rome.

TAKE YOUR SEATS

Rome had had a permanent amphitheater for gladiator shows since 29 B.C., but by A.D. 80 only an immense ring the size of the Colosseum could accommodate the eager crowds. Around 45,000 could be seated, with standing room for another 5,000 people. An awning of canvas protected them from the sun, and a metal grille around the vast, sand-filled arena protected them from the carnage in the ring.

FINAL DECISION
A triumphant gladiator looks up to the emperor and waits for a sign to finish off his opponent. The emperor would often let the crowd decide. If the defeated gladiator had fought bravely, they might take pity on him.

SEA BATTLES

The Colosseum was engineered so that its arena could be flooded with water. On this artificial lake, a mock naval battle could be staged. The ships were small versions of naval ships used by the Roman army, manned by teams of gladiators. Wild crocodiles were shipped in to swim in the lake as an extra hazard for gladiators to face if they fell in!

WILD BEASTS

During the reign of Trajan, the flooding mechanisms beneath the Colosseum were replaced with compartments for wild animals. Elephants, lions, bears, wolves, and rhinoceroses were tormented and released to fight each other. Often they were set upon humans, such as condemned criminals. Men, women, and children were savaged to death.

UNDERGROUND MAZE
Wild animals and prisoners were caged in the maze of tunnels beneath the Colosseum. From here, they could be winched up to the arena and released in front of the roaring crowd.

AN AWESOME STRUCTURE
The Colosseum was designed rather like a modern soccer stadium with rows of seats arranged in tiers around the ring. It had eighty entrance arches at ground level.

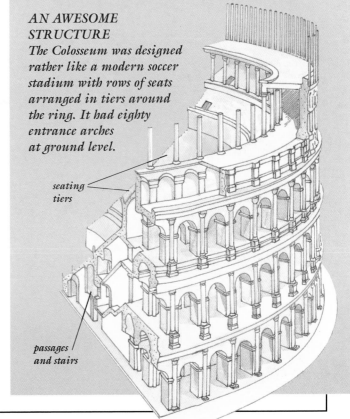

seating tiers

passages and stairs

OUT OF AFRICA
Many wild animal species became extinct in North Africa under Roman rule because so many were being shipped to Rome for shows. The emperor Trajan celebrated his Dacian campaign, A.D. 106, by killing 11,000 beasts.

THOSE ABOUT TO DIE

Fights between gladiators were held in amphitheaters all over the Roman Empire and gamblers betted on the outcome. Although combat was brutal and bloody, pictures of it featured in home mosaics and decorated everyday items such as cups.

ONE LAST CHANCE

Gladiators were drawn from those in society who had nothing left to lose—mostly criminals, slaves, or prisoners of war. They were bought and sold by dealers and underwent strict training in barracks, such as the one discovered in Pompeii. Many of the gladiators had lived and trained together before they met in the ring. A few became famous fighters, admired by the audience, and these would return to the arena time after time. Most, however, met a wretched death as the crowds chanted "kill!"

WOMEN GLADIATORS
Most gladiators were men, but we do know that women occasionally fought in the ring. This marble engraving of "Amazons" (named after the female fighters of Greek legend) comes from Bodrum, Turkey, and is dated between the 1st and 2nd century A.D.

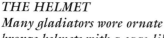

THE HELMET
Many gladiators wore ornate bronze helmets with a cage-like visor covering the face. The design was based on the armor of the Samnites, a hill people from southern Italy.

PICTURES OF DEATH
Although combat was brutal and deadly, it was pictured on frescoes and mosaics in the home, as well as on many everyday items.

NETS AND TRIDENTS

Each type of gladiator was named after his type of armor, weapons, or style of fighting. For example, the "reticarius" was armed with a trident, or three-pronged spear, and a net. while the "secutor" had a short sword and shield. Others, such as Britons, Gauls, or Thracians were named after the area where they were taken prisoner. They wore their regional costume and used their own weapons.

DEATH IN THE ARENA

If a defeated gladiator had fought bravely, the emperor bowed to the wishes of the crowd and granted him his life. Gladiators who lay dying were executed by a figure with a black-painted face, dressed as a demon of the underworld. Corpses were hauled from the arena and treated no better than the animals.

A FIGHT TO THE DEATH
Hundreds of gladiators might perform in a show. Before the combat began they would turn to the emperor with the words "Those who are about to die, salute you!" They were indeed trained to die. Only the most successful gladiators survived more than a few weeks of combat.

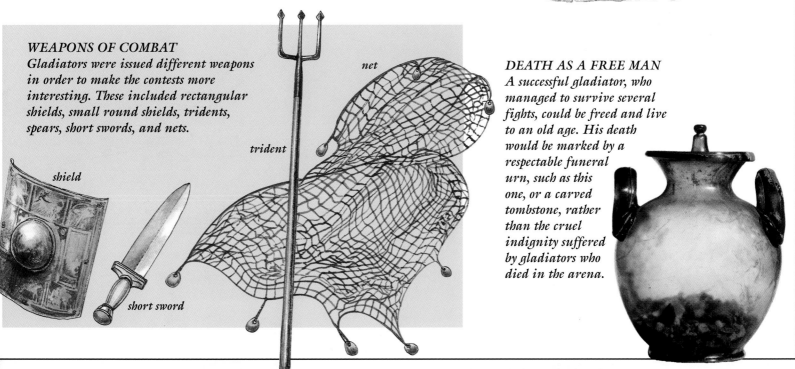

WEAPONS OF COMBAT
Gladiators were issued different weapons in order to make the contests more interesting. These included rectangular shields, small round shields, tridents, spears, short swords, and nets.

net

trident

shield

short sword

DEATH AS A FREE MAN
A successful gladiator, who managed to survive several fights, could be freed and live to an old age. His death would be marked by a respectable funeral urn, such as this one, or a carved tombstone, rather than the cruel indignity suffered by gladiators who died in the arena.

49

LAST DAYS OF ROME

In the third and fourth centuries A.D., the Roman Empire began to lose its hold on Europe. Local governors tried to seize power for themselves, while from the outside, warriors began to test Roman defenses along the frontiers of the Empire.

A CHRISTIAN EMPEROR

In A.D. 286, the emperor Diocletian divided the Roman Empire into an eastern and a western half in order to make it easier to govern. It was temporarily reunited in A.D. 324 by the emperor Constantine the Great. Constantine was the first Roman emperor to become a Christian. Christianity, banned in Rome since the days of emperor Nero, now became the state religion. In A.D. 330 Constantine built a new city to rival Rome, called Constantinople, on the site of ancient Byzantium (modern Istanbul), and chose it as his new capital.

DECLINE AND FALL
There were many causes for the downfall of Rome. The simple ideals of Rome's early days were forgotten. Many rulers preferred lives of luxury, and were greedy, corrupt, and cruel. The Empire was becoming too expensive to run, and distant wars in Asia were pushing warlike tribes westward into Europe. Altogether, it was a recipe for disaster.

CONSTANTINE THE GREAT
The reign of Constantine, was marked by bitter rivalry and civil war due to the introduction of a new center of the Empire and a new religion.

UNDER ATTACK

Enemies of Rome began to overrun Rome's frontiers. Britain was attacked by Irish raiders in the west and by Germanic tribes called Angles and Saxons in the east, and many wealthy Romans buried their wealth to hide it from marauding bands. A new string of stone forts, known as the "Saxon shore," was built to defend southeast England. By A.D. 406, the Roman legions had withdrawn from Britain— it was no longer part of the Empire. Meanwhile, Germanic tribes such as the Franks pushed westward into Gaul.

THE BITTER END

In A.D. 410 a band of warriors from Germany, called Goths, invaded Italy itself and plundered the city of Rome before moving into other parts of the Empire including Gaul (France) and Spain. In A.D. 455 a Vandal army from Germany again attacked Rome. The Empire in the west finally collapsed in A.D. 476 when the last emperor, Romulus Augustulus, was overthrown by more German invaders. A barbarian (a Greek term adopted into the Roman language) tribe finally established a Germanic kingdom in Italy around A.D. 493. The eastern part of the Empire survived for almost a thousand years more, but based so far from Rome, it was soon dominated by Greek language and culture.

FIERCE ENEMIES
The Goths (shown as the enemy in this Roman stone frieze, above), were a group of powerful Germanic tribes who relentlessly attacked the Roman Empire for more than 200 years.

CHRISTIANITY
Once adopted officially as a new religion, Christianity spread rapidly through the Empire.

THE ROMAN LEGACY

From the fifth century A.D., *Rome was in the hands of people who had once lived outside the borders of the Roman Empire—people who had once been despised as uncivilized barbarians. Across Europe, unrepaired roads turned back into muddy tracks and cities were burnt down and abandoned. However, Roman civilization, and its culture and architecture, was not forgotten.*

LANGUAGE AND LAW

The thousand years after the fall of Rome are known as the Middle Ages. In this period the city regained its greatness, this time as a center of the Christian faith. The language of the Church remained Latin, as spoken in ancient Rome, and Latin was still spoken by scholars throughout Europe. The surviving eastern (or Byzantine) Empire adopted and developed Roman law. This is still the basis of the legal system in many countries around the world today.

THE LIGHTHOUSE
The remains of a Roman lighthouse still tower over the port of Dover in southern England. Once a beacon of Roman power and a watchtower against Saxon raiders, it was later used as the bell tower for a Christian church. More than thirty lighthouses are known to have been built by the Romans.

CHRISTIAN FUTURE
This arch was erected in honor of Constantine I after he won the battle of the Milvian Bridge in A.D. *312. During this battle, Constantine claimed to see a vision of the Christian cross in the sky. A miracle or not, Rome's future would certainly be Christian.*

REDISCOVERY

After the Middle Ages, there was a great *renaissance* (rebirth) of learning, art, and science in Western Europe. People rediscovered the poets, artists, and thinkers of ancient Greece and Rome, and began to appreciate their culture and way of life. In the 1600s, 1700s, and 1800s, Europeans looked back to Rome for inspiration when they built up new nations and empires.

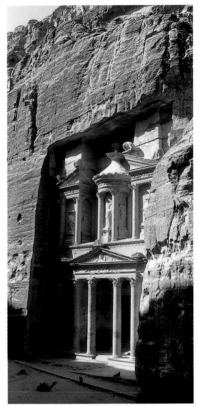

ROCK SOLID
The Roman treasury in Petra, Jordan, is carved from the desert rockface. The city of Petra was captured from Nabataean Arabs in A.D. 106.

THE FORUM
The remains of a forum in Libya (below) reveal that Rome was shaping its Empire into an economic and political union nearly 2,000 years before the European Union was established.

MAGNIFICENT ARCHITECTURE
The sheer scale of the Lepcis Theater in Libya still takes our breath away 2,000 years after it was built. Civil engineering was one of the greatest achievements of Roman civilization.

INSPIRING RUINS

One reason that people could never forget the Romans was the fact that their buildings survived. Some were plundered for their stone, some were ruined, but all over the former Empire, magnificent bridges, city walls, temples, and aqueducts were still standing as testimony to its past might.

HISTORY IN STONE

The ancient sites of Pompeii and nearby Herculaneum were rediscovered and began to be excavated in the 1700s. Ever since then, archaeologists have been piecing together the true story of ancient Rome from the evidence collected.

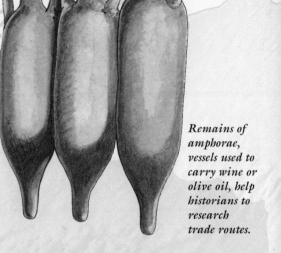

Remains of amphorae, vessels used to carry wine or olive oil, help historians to research trade routes.

Many mighty Roman structures are still standing, 2,000 years later.

Remains of soldiers' uniforms have been discovered throughout the old Empire.

ARCHAEOLOGISTS AT WORK

Archaeology is painstaking work. All over the former Roman Empire, vital clues have been uncovered, aided by modern technology. Radio-carbon analysis helps scientists to date fragments of wood or textile. Scientists can determine diet, health, and even working conditions by studying human bones. Computer models and calculations make it possible to recreate images of ruined buildings.

Milestones mark the route of old Roman roads.

A cache of coins found in southern Britain.

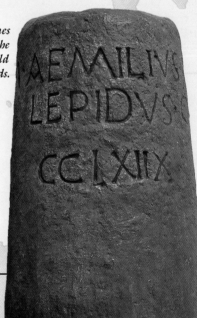

AEMILIVS
LEPIDVS
CCLXIIX

LAND, SEA, AND AIR

Aerial photography has helped archaeologists discover long-buried forts or Roman roads, and to compare modern field patterns with those of ancient times. Diving technology has made it possible for us to discover scores of Roman shipwrecks around the coasts of Europe. By examining amphorae (pottery containers) of oil or wine, often stamped with the trader's name, experts can work out Roman trading patterns. Remnants of red earthernware from North Africa dating back to the first and second centuries A.D. have been found throughout Rome.

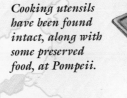

Cooking utensils have been found intact, along with some preserved food, at Pompeii.

Roman murals and carved friezes often focused on everyday scenes.

Materials such as ivory and marble have survived through the years.

THE WRITTEN WORD

The Romans were excellent writers and historians. Julius Caesar's accounts of his wars in Gaul (France) provide an insight into the world in which he lived, although one person's account may not always represent the whole truth. British archaeologists have uncovered many written fragments from forts along Hadrian's Wall. There are letters from soldiers about their socks and a lady's party invitation. These give us glimpses into the lives of the ordinary people who helped to create the Roman Empire.

Ancient mosaics have been uncovered under old buildings and sand.

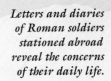

Letters and diaries of Roman soldiers stationed abroad reveal the concerns of their daily life.

TIME LINE OF ANCIENT ROME

753 B.C.
According to legend, Rome is founded in 753 B.C.

700 B.C.
Greeks colonize parts of Italy and Sicily, bringing their culture and religion.

715–509 B.C
Rome is under the rule of an Etruscan monarchy.

509 B.C.
Romans eject the Etruscan rulers and set up a Republic with elected consuls.

493 B.C.
Plebians (ordinary people of Rome) have officers called tribunes, to look after their interests.

Settlements are built on some of the seven hills along the River Tiber.

The first settlers live in wooden huts around th Palatine Hill.

circa 200 B.C.
Romans use concrete for the first time, and the first three-storey insulae are built in Rome for working-class people.

149–146 B.C.
Third Punic War. Carthage and Corinth are destroyed. Rome becomes the major power in the Mediterranean.

140 B.C.
The 57-mile-long Aqua Marcia is the first aqueduct to have sections carried on arches.

85 B.C.
The hypocaust under-floor heating system is invented for use in villas, then used in public baths.

58–48 B.C.
Julius Caesar conquers France, and in 49 B.C. is made a "dictator for life," Rome's first sole ruler since 509 B.C.

218–202 B.C. General Hannibal, from Carthage, North Africa, and his 40,000 troops cross the Alps with forty elephants to attack Italy. He is defeated in A.D. 202.

A.D. 80
The Colosseum is finished under emperor Titus. It had been started ten years earlier by the emperor Vespasian.

A.D. 114
Trajan has a marble column built (Trajan's Column) to celebrate his military victories.

A.D. 117
Trajan is succeeded by Hadrian (to A.D. 138). The Roman Empire is at its height.

A.D. 130
Work is started on the Pantheon, the shrine to all of the gods, under orders of Hadrian.

A.D. 293
Emperor Diocletian splits the empire into an eastern half (province) and a western half.

A.D. 79 The volcano Vesuvius erupts, killing 20,000 people in Pompeii and Herculaneum.

A.D. 112 Hadrian's Wall takes ten years to build in northern Britain and is seventy-eight miles long.

400 B.C.
4th century B.C. Many public buildings and temples are erected.

312 B.C.
Work begins on the Via Appia, a road that will run from Rome to Brindisi on the coast.

290 B.C.
End of Samnite war—Rome wins control of central Italy and soon controls most of Italy.

264–241 B.C.
First war overseas—with the Carthaginians (or Phoenicians), in North Africa (the Punic Wars).

218–202 B.C.
Second Punic War against Carthaginians in North Africa. Hannibal is defeated.

4th century A.D. Rome's forum begins to develop as an important meeting place for trade and worship.

312 B.C. Construction of the first aqueduct, the Aqua Appia, brings water to Rome.

42 B.C.
Statesmen Mark Antony and Octavian kill rivals Brutus and Cassius, in order to share power of the Senate.

40–27 B.C.
Antony is involved with Cleopatra, queen of Egypt. The pair are defeated by Octavian, Rome's first emperor.

A.D 43
Emperor Claudius leads a force of legions into Britain and captures its capital, Colchester.

A.D. 60
The Britons revolt against Roman rule led by Queen Boudicca (of the Iceni tribe). They are defeated. Boudicca kills herself.

A.D. 63–64
The Great Fire of Rome. Nero blames Christians for it and puts many to death.

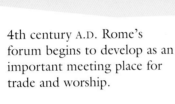

44 B.C. On March 15th, Cassius, Brutus, and other senators kill Julius Caesar.

27 B.C. Octavian (right) renames himself Augustus Caesar. He is the first emperor of Rome.

A.D. 330
Constantine establishes a new Christian capital, Constantinople. Rome is still the western capital.

A.D. 410
The Goths (German warriors) invade the Western Empire and capture Rome.

A.D. 415–452
German Visigoths, Vandals, and Huns take over parts of the Roman Empire.

A.D. 455
Rome falls into the hands of the Vandals and parts of the Western Empire are taken by barbarian rulers.

A.D. 476
Romulus Augustulus, ousted by a barbarian, is the last emperor of the Western Empire.

A.D 313 Constantine issues the Edict of Milan, allowing Christian worship.

A.D. 452 Attila the Hun attempts to invade Italy but is turned back by the Roman Army.

GLOSSARY

A

adze Type of hammer used by Roman boatwrights and builders.

amphitheater An oval arena, surrounded by seats, where shows were performed.

Amphorae

amphorae Large pottery containers used to transport wine or olive oil.

aqueduct Channels supported on arches that were used to carry water.

archaeologists People who study the past by examining remains of old buildings and things found in them.

architecture Design and structure of buildings.

augurs Officials who believed they could detect the movements and wishes of the gods.

auxiliaries Soldiers who were non-Roman citizens.

B

barbarians People from outside the Roman Empire, whom the Romans saw as uncivilized.

Emperor Caligula

C

capital Decorative design at the top of a column.

consul Leaders of the Senate; there were two elected annually by members of the Senate.

crucifixion Nailing a person to a wooden cross and usually leaving them to die there—a favored Roman punishment for criminals.

D

dictator A ruler who is not restricted by laws, and has no opposition.

domus Roman term for a private home, which was usually large with several rooms built around an inner courtyard.

E

emperors The people who ruled Rome in the days of the Empire.

Empire The area ruled by an emperor of Rome (from B.C. 27—A.D. 476).

Etruscans A group of people who controlled most of Italy from the 8th century B.C.

F

forum A business and shopping center, often a square in the middle of stores and offices.

fresco Painting made directly onto plaster on a wall.

G

Gaul The name for a large region of France in the Roman times.

gladiators The slaves who were trained to fight in the Colosseum and other arenas of ancient Rome.

Mars, the god of war

gods and goddesses Supernatural beings worshiped by people, and thought to control some aspect of life or the universe.

groma Instrument used for checking right angles in road building and engineering.

H

hypocaust An underfloor heating system.

I

insulae (islands) The blocks of apartments where the ordinary working class citizens of Rome lived.

L

Latin The language of ancient Rome and the Roman Empire.

legionaries Soldiers who were Roman citizens.

M

mortar and pestle Small pottery bowl (mortar) and a heavy, pottery club-shaped tool (pestle) used for grinding up herbs and spices in cooking.

mosaic A pattern made of tiny pieces of colored glass, stone, or pottery used to decorate a floor or wall.

mural Large wall painting.

P

papyrus Paper made from the stem of a reed-like water plant.

patricians Wealthy, aristocratic members of society.

Pax Romana It means Roman peace and was a term used to describe the years of stability under Augustus (Octavian), the very first emperor of Rome.

pecunia The name given to money in ancient Rome. Its name was derived from the Latin word for sheep.

Penates Spirits whom the Romans believed to look after their homes.

Persia Modern Iran.

plebians Ordinary poor people.

Pompeii An ancient city in southeast Italy, which was buried by lava from an erupting volcano, Vesuvius, in A.D. 79. Excavation of

Mosaic

Pompeii began in 1748. It is extremely well preserved and provides a wealth of information in the form of buildings, streets, and artifacts, showing how people lived in ancient Rome.

Praetorian Guard Personal bodyguards of the emperor and an elite group of well-paid soldiers.

princeps A term meaning "first citizen" which Augustus (Octavian) the first emperor, chose to call himself when he took control.

province Part of an Empire or a country, similar to a state.

R

Renaissance Period following the Middle Ages, around the 14th century, when people began taking a renewed interest in the arts and culture of ancient Greece and Rome.

Republic A form of government where representatives are elected to run the country.

Trident and net

S

Samnite Person belonging to a tribe, or group of people, from southern Italy.

Senate Rome's government.

stola Shawl worn by Roman women.

strigil Blade used to scrape oil off the body at baths.

stucco Decorative plaster moldings stuck onto walls or ceilings, originally made from a mixture of powdered marble, lime, and glue.

stylus Pointed tool used for engraving and drawing on a wax tablet.

Strigil

T

tesserae Small cubes of pottery, stone, glass, and tiles that were used to make mosaics.

toga Garment worn by wealthy and middle-class Romans, which was a long length of fabric draped around the body.

tribune Officers of the Senate elected to look after the interests of ordinary citizens of Rome.

trident Three-pronged fork used as a weapon.

V

villa Luxurious Roman country house usually richly decorated with mosaics and murals.

INDEX

PHOTO CREDITS

Key: a = above, b = below, c = center, l = left, r = right.